I'M THAT KID PRESENTS

TEACHING TEENS ABOUT MULTIPLE STREAMS OF INCOME

TRAY-SEAN BEN SALMI
AKA I'M THAT KID

I'M THAT KID PRESENTS

TEACHING TEENS ABOUT MULTIPLE STREAMS OF INCOME

Published by Influencer Publishing

PAPERBACK ISBN: 978-1-913310-89-9
HARDBACK ISBN: 978-1-913310-88-2

I'M THAT KID PRESENTS

TEACHING TEENS ABOUT MULTIPLE STREAMS OF INCOME

Always Remember
*There are an
abundance of
opportunities on
your doorstep.*

ACKNOWLEDGEMENTS

ACKNOWLEDGEMENTS

I would like to acknowledge you, the reader, for choosing to embark on this journey with me. As the saying goes… a journey of a thousand miles begins with a single step in the right direction; imagine how much you will shift once you've finished reading this book. I would also like to take this opportunity to acknowledge my family, friends, the team at Influencer Publishing, mentors and all of those who support and encourage me behind the scenes.

DEDICATION

DEDICATION

I dedicate this book to young people who refuse to give up and constantly strive to become the best they can be. I also dedicate this book to the parents who do their best to support their children. Life isn't always easy, so I dedicate this book to transforming your financial situation by expanding your awareness of an abundance of opportunities.

I also dedicate this book to those who have had to fight for financial stability and security; this book is dedicated to you. Your struggles and determination have inspired me to write about the importance of financial education and empowerment. With the knowledge and skills gained from this book, you will be able to overcome the obstacles that come with financial insecurity and build a brighter future for yourselves and your loved ones. I believe in your strength and resilience, and I am honoured to be a small part of your journey towards financial freedom.

INTRODUCTION

INTRODUCTION

This book aims to inspire young people to dream big and share insights about multiple streams of income that young people can explore. In 2022 I launched a new program called "I'm That KID - Teaching Teens How To Trade", which aims to teach young people how to trade stocks and shares. I enjoyed the vibe in the room while teaching. I led groups aged 8 to 11 year-olds and 12 to 15 year-olds, consisting of around 45-50 individuals. During a group discussion, I asked the group of 8 to 11-year-olds to call out different ways they could make money..., and to my dismay, the following answers were called out by a few eight years olds:

- Benefit
- Stealing
- Betting shop

Can you remember a time in your life when you were caught off guard and totally rendered speechless for a moment?... it was at that moment that I realised that the world I'm doing is deeply needed to revive hope and to recondition the hearts and minds of young people. I am a true believer in the power of influence. As a leader, I am committed to transforming the narrative of financial education for young people from deprived backgrounds, which inspired me to write this book. I am not a financial advisor, and I advise that you seek permission from your parent or guardian before actioning the examples in this book.

MULTIPLE STREAMS OF INCOME

MULTIPLE STREAMS OF INCOME

There are potentially an unlimited number of streams of income that a person could have. Some examples of streams of income might include:

- Earned income from a job or business
- Profit Income from goods or services
- Interest & dividends from investments
- Rental income from owning property
- Royalties from published work or intellectual property
- Pension or retirement income
- Gifts or inheritances

The number and type of streams of income a person has will depend on their individual circumstances and financial goals.

EARNED INCOME

EARNED INCOME

Earned income is any income that is received from a job, self-employment or business. This tends to be your primary stream of income. The majority of us start here, and many go no further. For most, earned income is very limiting and has attracted the acronym, 'Just Over Broke!'.

In other words, you earn just enough to survive; some jobs pay exceptionally well, but these are exceptions, not the norm. To go beyond a job and start your own business requires taking risks and moving into other income streams.

Are you looking for a business account that adapts to your needs? Penta offers you an all-inclusive package. There are several types of earned income, including wages, salaries, commissions, tips, and self-employment income. Wages are typically paid by the hour, while salaries are paid on a regular basis, such as weekly, biweekly, or monthly. The commission is income that is earned based on the sale of a product or service. Service industry workers such as waiters, hairdressers, and taxi drivers often earn tips. Self-employment income is earned by those who are self-employed, such as freelancers or business owners.

EARNED INCOME

There are several types of earned income, including:

- Wages: These are typically paid by the hour and may be earned through employment or through self-employment.

- Salaries: These are typically paid on a regular basis, such as weekly, biweekly, or monthly, and may be earned through employment or through self-employment.

- Commission: This is income that is earned based on the sale of a product or service. It may be earned through employment or through self-employment.

- Tips: These are often earned by service industry workers such as waiters, hairdressers, and taxi drivers.

- Self-employment income: This is earned by those who are self-employed, such as freelancers or business owners.

If you listen, you will learn and if you learn you will earn.

I challenge you to do research and then develop a plan to plant a seed toward increasing your earned income.

_____

_____

_____

_____

_____

_____

_____

_____

_____

_____

_____

_____

_____

NOTES

MULTIPLE STREAMS OF INCOME

_____

_____

_____

_____

_____

_____

_____

_____

_____

_____

_____

_____

_____

PROFIT
INCOME

PROFIT INCOME

Profit income is the income that a person or business receives from selling goods or services at a price higher than the cost of producing them. For a business, profit is an important indicator of financial performance, as it represents the excess revenue available to be reinvested in the business or distributed to shareholders as dividends.

Profit is calculated by subtracting the costs of producing goods or services (including expenses such as labour, materials, and overhead) from the revenue generated from their sale. For an individual, profit income might come from the sale of goods or services that they produce and sell, such as crafts or home-baked goods. It could also come from the sale of assets, such as stocks or real estate if the sale price is higher than the original purchase price. Profit income is income that is earned from the ownership of a business or from investments.

There are several types of profit income, including:

- Dividend income: This is income that is paid to shareholders of a company's stock.

- Interest income: This is income earned from lending money, such as from a bank account or a bond.

PROFIT INCOME

- Rental income: This is income that is earned from the rental of property, such as a house or apartment.

- Capital gains are the profit made from selling an asset, such as stocks or real estate.

- Royalty income: This is income that is earned from the use of intellectual property, such as a patent or a copyrighted work.

Under promise and over deliver. Always deliver more than expected.

I challenge you to do research and then develop a plan to plant a seed toward increasing your profit income.

_____

_____

_____

_____

_____

_____

_____

_____

_____

_____

_____

_____

_____

_____

_____

NOTES

MULTIPLE STREAMS OF INCOME

INTEREST & DIVIDEND INCOME

INTEREST & DIVIDEND INCOME

Interest income is money earned from a financial investment, such as a savings account, certificate of deposit (CD), or bond. When you invest money in a financial product that pays interest, the issuer of the product (such as a bank or government) will pay you a percentage of the principal (the original amount of money invested) as interest over a certain period of time.

Dividend income is money paid to shareholders of a company as a distribution of the company's profits. If you own stocks in a company, you may be entitled to receive dividends on a regular basis (usually quarterly). Dividends can be paid in the form of cash, additional shares of stock, or other property. Like interest income, dividend income is a stream of passive income, meaning that it is generated without the need for active work or effort on the part of the recipient.

There are several types of interest and dividend income:

- Simple interest: This is interest that is paid on the principal amount of a loan or investment. The interest rate is fixed, and the interest is paid at regular intervals, such as monthly or annually.

INTEREST & DIVIDEND INCOME

- Compound interest: This is interest that is paid on both the principal amount of a loan or investment and the accumulated interest. The interest rate is fixed, and the interest is compounded at regular intervals, such as monthly or annually.
- Ordinary dividends: These are dividends that are paid out of a company's profits. They are typically paid in cash or stock.
- Qualified dividends: These are dividends that are paid by domestic or qualified foreign corporations and are taxed at the capital gains tax rate rather than the ordinary income tax rate.
- Non-qualified dividends: These are dividends that do not meet the requirements to be classified as qualified dividends and are taxed at the ordinary income tax rate.

Successful investing is about managing risk, not avoiding it.

I challenge you to do research and then develop a plan to plant a seed toward increasing your interest and dividend income.

_____

_____

_____

_____

_____

_____

_____

_____

_____

_____

_____

_____

_____

NOTES

MULTIPLE STREAMS OF INCOME

_____

_____

_____

_____

_____

_____

_____

_____

_____

_____

_____

_____

_____ MULTIPLE STREAMS OF INCOME

RENTAL
INCOME

RENTAL INCOME

Rental income is money that is received from renting out a property, such as an apartment, house, or office space. If you own a rental property and have tenants living in it, you will receive rental income from the monthly rent payments made by the tenants. Rental income can be a good source of passive income, as it is generated from the property without the need for active work or effort on the part of the owner. However, it is important to keep in mind that owning rental property also involves responsibilities and costs, such as maintaining the property, paying taxes, and possibly paying for a property management company.

There are several different types of rental income that an individual or business might receive. Some examples include:

- Residential rental income: This is income received from renting out a house, apartment, or other residential property to individuals or families.

- Commercial rental income is income received from renting out a property, such as an office building or retail space, to businesses.

RENTAL INCOME

- Vacation rental income: This is income received from renting out a property, such as a vacation home or apartment, to travellers on a short-term basis (usually less than a month).

- Self-storage rental income is income from renting out storage units to individuals or businesses.

- Equipment rental income: This is income received from renting out equipment, such as construction machinery or party supplies, to individuals or businesses.

There may also be other types of rental income, depending on the property or assets being rented out.

Don't wait to buy real estate,
buy real estate and wait.

I challenge you to do research and then develop a plan to plant a seed toward increasing your rental income.

_____

_____

_____

_____

_____

_____

_____

_____

_____

_____

_____

_____

_____

NOTES

MULTIPLE STREAMS OF INCOME

ROYALTY INCOME

ROYALTY INCOME

Royalty income is a payment made to someone for the use of a copyrighted work, natural resource, or other intellectual property. It is usually a percentage of the sales or profits that are generated from the use of the property. For example, an author might receive a royalty on the sale of each copy of a book that they have written, or a musician might receive a royalty on the sale of each record or CD that contains their music. Royalty income is typically paid to the owner of the property that is being used, such as an author or a musician. Still, it can also be paid to a licensing agency or other intermediaries that has the right to license the use of the property on behalf of the owner.

There are many different types of royalty income, as the concept of royalty income can be applied to various types of intellectual property and natural resources. Some common types of royalty income include:

- Copyright royalties: These are payments made for the use of a copyrighted work, such as a book, song, or photograph.

- Patent royalties: These are payments made for the use of a patented invention or product.

- Trademark royalties: These are payments made for the use of a trademarked brand or logo.

ROYALTY INCOME

- Mineral royalties: These are payments made for the extraction and sale of minerals, such as oil, gas, or coal.

- Timber royalties: These are payments made for the sale of timber from forested land.

- Licensing fees: These are payments made for the right to use a copyrighted work, patented product, or trademarked brand.

There are many other types of royalty income as well, depending on the specific type of intellectual property or a natural resource that is being licensed.

Everything changes for the better with ownership.

I challenge you to do research and then develop a plan to plant a seed toward increasing your royalty income.

_____

_____

_____

_____

_____

_____

_____

_____

_____

_____

_____

_____

_____

_____

NOTES
MULTIPLE STREAMS OF INCOME

PENSION AND RETIREMENT INCOME

PENSION AND RETIREMENT INCOME

Pension income is income received from a pension plan, a retirement savings plan sponsored by an employer or a union. A pension plan provides a guaranteed stream of income to an employee after they retire.

Retirement income is any income that is received during retirement, including pension income, social security income, and income from retirement savings accounts such as 401(k)s and individual retirement accounts (IRAs). Retirement income can also include income from part-time work or from rental property.

There are several types of pension and retirement income:

- Defined benefit pension: This is a type of pension plan in which the employer guarantees a certain level of income to the employee after they retire. The amount of the pension is based on factors such as the employee's salary, length of service, and age at retirement.

- Defined contribution pension: This is a type of pension plan in which the employer makes contributions to the employee's pension account, and the employee's retirement income is based on the balance in their account. Examples of defined contribution pension plans include 401(k) plans and individual retirement accounts (IRAs).

PENSION AND RETIREMENT INCOME

- Social Security: This is a federally-administered retirement program that provides a guaranteed stream of income to eligible workers and their families.

- Income from retirement savings accounts: This is income that is received from retirement savings accounts such as 401(k)s and IRAs. The income may come in the form of withdrawals or through the use of annuities.

- Income from part-time work: Some people choose to work part-time during retirement in order to supplement their retirement income.

- Income from rental property: Some people choose to invest in rental property as a source of retirement income.

If you fail to plan, you're ultimately planning to fail.

I challenge you to do research and then develop a plan to plant a seed toward increasing your pension and retirement income.

_____

_____

_____

_____

_____

_____

_____

_____

_____

_____

_____

_____

NOTES

MULTIPLE STREAMS OF INCOME

_____

_____

_____

_____

_____

_____

_____

_____

_____

_____

_____

_____

_____ MULTIPLE STREAMS OF INCOME

GIFTS, CAPITAL GAINS & INHERITANCE INCOME

GIFTS, CAPITAL GAINS & INHERITANCE INCOME

Gift income is income that is received in the form of a gift, such as cash or property. Gifts are not considered taxable income for the recipient, unless the gift is in the form of income-producing property, such as rental property or stocks.

Capital gains income is the profit that is realized from the sale of a capital asset, such as stocks, real estate, or collectibles. Capital gains are subject to taxation, and the tax rate depends on the type of asset and the length of time it was held.

Inheritance income is income that is received as a result of inheriting property, such as cash, stocks, or real estate, from someone who has passed away. Inheritances are not considered taxable income for the recipient. However, if the inherited property generates income, such as rental income or dividends, that income may be subject to taxation.

There are several types of gifts, capital gains, and inheritance income:

- Cash gifts: These are gifts of cash or other monetary instruments, such as checks or money orders.

- Property gifts: These are gifts of property, such as real estate, art, or collectibles.

GIFTS, CAPITAL GAINS & INHERITANCE INCOME

- Long-term capital gains: These are capital gains that are realized from the sale of a capital asset that was held for more than one year. Long-term capital gains are generally taxed at a lower rate than short-term capital gains.

- Short-term capital gains: These are capital gains that are realized from the sale of a capital asset that was held for one year or less. Short-term capital gains are generally taxed at a higher rate than long-term capital gains.

- Inheritance of cash or other monetary instruments: This is inheritance of cash or other monetary instruments, such as checks or money orders.

- Inheritance of property: This is inheritance of property, such as real estate, art, or collectables.

- Inheritance of a business: This is inheritance of a business, such as a sole proprietorship, partnership, or corporation.

- Inheritance of a trust: This is inheritance of an interest in a trust, which is a legal arrangement in which a person (the grantor) transfers ownership of property to another person (the trustee) to hold and manage for the benefit of a third person (the beneficiary).

Consistency transforms
mediocracy into excellence.

I challenge you to do research and then develop a plan to plant a seed toward increasing your gifts, capital gains & inheritance income.

_____

_____

_____

_____

_____

_____

_____

_____

_____

_____

_____

_____

NOTES
MULTIPLE STREAMS OF INCOME

EXAMPLES OF MULTIPLE STREAMS OF INCOME

EXAMPLES OF MULTIPLE STREAMS OF INCOME

Having multiple streams of income is an important financial strategy for anyone looking to secure their financial future and protect themselves from financial uncertainty. Having multiple sources of income allows you to diversify your income and reduce your reliance on any one source of income. This can provide a cushion in the event that one of your income streams experiences a downturn, as you will still have other sources of income to fall back on.

There are several reasons why having multiple streams of income is important:

1. Financial security: Having multiple streams of income can provide a sense of financial security and stability. If you rely on just one source of income and that source dries up, you could be in financial trouble. However, if you have multiple streams of income, you have a backup plan in place and you are less likely to be caught off guard by financial challenges.
2. Increased income: Having multiple streams of income can also lead to an overall increase in income. This is because each stream of income has the potential to contribute to your overall income. For example, if you have a full-time job that pays $50,000 per year and you also have a part-time job that pays $10,000 per year, your total income is $60,000 per year.
3. Career flexibility: Multiple streams of income can also provide career flexibility. If you have multiple sources of income, you have the option to pursue your passions and interests without the pressure of relying on a single source of income. This can lead to increased job satisfaction and a sense of control over your financial future.

It is generally recommended to have at least one to three streams of income. This allows you to diversify your income and reduce your reliance

EXAMPLES OF MULTIPLE STREAMS OF INCOME

on any one source of income. Some examples of potential streams of income include a full-time or part-time job, a side hustle or freelance work, rental income from a property, or income from investments. In conclusion, having multiple streams of income is an important financial strategy for anyone looking to secure their financial future and protect themselves from financial uncertainty. It can provide financial security, increased income, and career flexibility. It is recommended to have at least one to three streams of income to diversify your income and reduce your reliance on any one source.

Here are 40 ideas for generating multiple streams of income:

- Rent out a room on Airbnb
- Sell products on an e-commerce platform like Etsy or Amazon
- Offer tutoring or teaching services
- Create and sell an online course
- Sell print-on-demand products through a platform like Printful
- Invest in stocks or other securities
- Rent out your car or bike through a platform like Turo or Spinlister
- Offer pet-sitting or dog-walking services
- Rent out your tools or equipment
- Offer photography or videography services
- Sell handmade or unique products at craft fairs or markets
- Offer lawn care or landscaping services
- Rent out your parking space
- Offer social media marketing services
- Sell digital products like ebooks or printables
- Offer transcription or translation services
- Invest in rental properties
- Offer web design or development services

- Sell your skills as a freelancer
- Offer accounting or bookkeeping services
- Invest in a small business or franchise
- Sell your art or other creative work
- Offer event planning or coordination services
- Rent out your spare storage space
- Invest in a high-yield savings account or CD
- Offer consulting services in your area of expertise
- Sell your own branded merchandise
- Invest in a peer-to-peer lending platform
- Offer personal training or fitness coaching services
- Rent out your equipment or tools to other professionals
- Sell your skills as a virtual assistant
- Invest in cryptocurrency
- Sell your own branded meal prep or catering services
- Offer home cleaning or organization services
- Rent out your home on a vacation rental platform like VRBO or HomeAway
- Sell your skills as a graphic designer
- Invest in a crowdfunding platform
- Offer voiceover services
- Sell your skills as a writer or editor
- Invest in a dropshipping business.

NOTES

MULTIPLE STREAMS OF INCOME

_____

_____

_____

_____

_____

_____

_____

_____

_____

_____

_____ MULTIPLE STREAMS OF INCOME

Always Remember
Whatever you can imagine is real; you have to call it into your life.

1-18 EXAMPLES OF MULTIPLE STREAMS OF INCOME EXPLAINED

1-18 EXAMPLES OF MULTIPLE STREAMS OF INCOME EXPLAINED

Allow me to briefly explain how you could go about taking action to start 1-18 out of the 40 examples that I have shared.

RENT OUT A ROOM ON AIRBNB

- Determine which room in your home is suitable for renting out

- Create a listing on Airbnb, including photos and a detailed description of the space

- Set your availability and pricing

- Welcome and communicate with guests during their stay

NOTES
MULTIPLE STREAMS OF INCOME

_____

_____

_____

_____

_____

_____

_____

_____

_____

_____

_____

SELL PRODUCTS ON AN E-COMMERCE PLATFORM LIKE ETSY OR AMAZON

- Identify a product or product line that you can sell online

- Set up a seller account on an e-commerce platform like Etsy or Amazon

- Create a listing for each product, including photos and a detailed description

- Set your pricing and shipping options

- Monitor your sales and fulfilment process

NOTES

MULTIPLE STREAMS OF INCOME

_____

_____

_____

_____

_____

_____

_____

_____

_____

_____

_____

_____

OFFER TUTORING OR TEACHING SERVICES

- Determine what subject or subjects you are qualified to teach

- Create a website or social media presence to advertise your services

- Set your hourly rate or package pricing

- Communicate with potential clients and schedule sessions

NOTES

MULTIPLE STREAMS OF INCOME

_____

_____

_____

_____

_____

_____

_____

_____

_____

_____

_____

_____

_____

CREATE AND SELL AN ONLINE COURSE

- Identify a subject or skill that you are knowledgeable about and can teach others

- Determine the format and structure of your course (e.g. video lectures, written modules, quizzes)

- Create and organize the content for your course

- Set up a platform for delivering your course (e.g. Teachable, Udemy)

- Market and promote your course to potential students

NOTES

MULTIPLE STREAMS OF INCOME

_____
_____
_____
_____
_____
_____
_____
_____
_____
_____
_____
_____
_____

SELL PRINT-ON-DEMAND PRODUCTS THROUGH A PLATFORM LIKE PRINTFUL

- Determine what type of product you want to sell (e.g. t-shirts, mugs, phone cases)

- Design your product using a tool like Adobe Illustrator or Canva

- Set up a seller account on a print-on-demand platform like Printful

- Create a listing for each product, including photos and a detailed description

- Set your pricing and shipping options

- Monitor your sales and fulfilment process

NOTES

MULTIPLE STREAMS OF INCOME

_____

_____

_____

_____

_____

_____

_____

_____

_____

_____

_____

INVEST IN STOCKS OR OTHER SECURITIES

- Research and choose a brokerage firm to open an account with

- Determine your investment goals and risk tolerance

- Educate yourself on the basics of investing in stocks or other securities

- Start small and diversify your portfolio

- Monitor your investments and adjust as needed

NOTES

MULTIPLE STREAMS OF INCOME

_____

_____

_____

_____

_____

_____

_____

_____

_____

_____

_____

_____

_____ MULTIPLE STREAMS OF INCOME

RENT OUT YOUR CAR OR BIKE THROUGH A PLATFORM LIKE TURO OR SPINLISTER

- Determine which vehicle(s) you are willing to rent out

- Set up a listing on a car or bike-sharing platforms like Turo or Spinlister

- Include photos and a detailed description of your vehicle

- Set your availability and pricing

- Communicate with and meet up with renters during the rental process

NOTES

MULTIPLE STREAMS OF INCOME

_____

_____

_____

_____

_____

_____

_____

_____

_____

_____

_____

_____

OFFER PET-SITTING OR DOG-WALKING SERVICES

- Determine your availability and service area

- Create a website or social media presence to advertise your services

- Set your hourly rate or package pricing

- Communicate with potential clients and schedule services

NOTES

MULTIPLE STREAMS OF INCOME

_____

_____

_____

_____

_____

_____

_____

_____

_____

_____

_____

_____

_____ MULTIPLE STREAMS OF INCOME

RENT OUT YOUR TOOLS OR EQUIPMENT

- Determine which tools or equipment you are willing to rent out

- Create a listing on a tool or equipment rental platform like EquipmentShare or Zilok

- Include photos and a detailed description of each item

- Set your availability and pricing

- Communicate with and meet up with renters during the rental process

NOTES

MULTIPLE STREAMS OF INCOME

OFFER PHOTOGRAPHY OR VIDEOGRAPHY SERVICES

- Determine your niche or speciality within photography or videography (e.g. wedding, event, product)

- Create a website or social media presence to advertise your services

- Set your hourly rate or package pricing

- Communicate

NOTES

MULTIPLE STREAMS OF INCOME

_____

_____

_____

_____

_____

_____

_____

_____

_____

_____

_____

_____

SELL HANDMADE OR UNIQUE PRODUCTS AT CRAFT FAIRS OR MARKETS

- Choose the products you want to sell and make sure they are of good quality.

- Create a brand and a cohesive look for your products.

- Set your prices and determine your profit margins.

- Research local craft fairs and markets to see if they are a good fit for your products.

- Apply to participate in the fairs or markets and secure a booth or table.

- Promote your products and the craft fairs or markets you will be attending.

NOTES

MULTIPLE STREAMS OF INCOME

_____

_____

_____

_____

_____

_____

_____

_____

_____

_____

_____

_____ MULTIPLE STREAMS OF INCOME

OFFER LAWN CARE OR LANDSCAPING SERVICES

- Consider getting certified or taking some courses to learn about best practices in lawn care and landscaping.

- Buy or rent the necessary equipment and supplies.

- Determine your rates and create a pricing structure.

- Promote your services to potential clients by creating flyers and/or a website.

NOTES

MULTIPLE STREAMS OF INCOME

RENT OUT YOUR PARKING SPACE

- Determine the price you want to charge for your parking space.

- Create a listing for your parking space on a platform like SpotHero or JustPark.

- Promote your parking space to potential renters.

NOTES

MULTIPLE STREAMS OF INCOME

_____

_____

_____

_____

_____

_____

_____

_____

_____

_____

_____

_____ MULTIPLE STREAMS OF INCOME

OFFER SOCIAL MEDIA MARKETING SERVICES

- Learn about social media marketing strategies and best practices.

- Build a portfolio of your work.

- Create a website or online platform to advertise your services.

- Determine your rates and create a pricing structure.

- Reach out to potential clients and let them know about your services.

NOTES

MULTIPLE STREAMS OF INCOME

SELL DIGITAL PRODUCTS LIKE EBOOKS OR PRINTABLES

- Choose the digital products you want to sell and create them.

- Determine your prices and profit margins.

- Set up a website or online store to sell your products.

- Promote your products through social media and other online channels.

NOTES

MULTIPLE STREAMS OF INCOME

OFFER TRANSCRIPTION OR TRANSLATION SERVICES

- Consider taking some courses or getting certified to improve your skills and learn about industry standards and best practices.

- Build a portfolio of your work.

- Create a website or online platform to advertise your services.

- Set your rates and figure out your pricing structure.

- Reach out to potential clients and let them know about your services.

NOTES

MULTIPLE STREAMS OF INCOME

INVEST IN RENTAL PROPERTIES

- Research the local real estate market to identify good investment opportunities.

- Determine your budget and financing options.

- Find and purchase a rental property.

- Set up a property management system, such as finding and screening tenants and handling maintenance and repairs.

NOTES

MULTIPLE STREAMS OF INCOME

OFFER WEB DESIGN OR DEVELOPMENT SERVICES

- Learn about web design and development techniques and best practices.

- Build a portfolio of your work.

- Create a website or online platform to advertise your services.

- Determine your rates and create a pricing structure.

- Reach out to potential clients and let them know about your services.

NOTES

MULTIPLE STREAMS OF INCOME

CONCLUSION

CONCLUSION

In conclusion, financial education is a powerful tool in the fight against poverty. By teaching individuals the skills and knowledge they need to make informed financial decisions, we can empower them to take control of their financial futures and break the cycle of poverty.

Financial education can provide people with the tools they need to create and manage a budget, save and invest for the future, and make informed decisions about credit and debt. It can also help people understand their rights and responsibilities as consumers, allowing them to protect themselves from financial scams and predatory lending practices.

Furthermore, financial education can help individuals build the skills and confidence they need to start their own businesses and create new streams of income. This can be especially important in communities where job opportunities are scarce or where individuals may face barriers to employment due to their socioeconomic status.

Overall, financial education is a crucial component of any strategy to combat poverty. By investing in financial education programs and initiatives, we can help individuals and communities build the skills and knowledge they need to achieve financial stability and prosperity.

The question is, how many income streams do you currently have? As a result of reading this book, how many income streams are you likely to create?

I encourage you to do your own research and commit to your financial liberation one step at a time.

Always Remember

That wealth is your birthright.

NOTES

MULTIPLE STREAMS OF INCOME

USE THE FOLLOWING PAGES TO
CREATE YOUR VERY OWN ACTION
PLAN.

NOTES

MULTIPLE STREAMS OF INCOME

NOTES

MULTIPLE STREAMS OF INCOME

_____

_____

_____

_____

_____

_____

_____

_____

_____

_____

_____

_____ MULTIPLE STREAMS OF INCOME

NOTES

MULTIPLE STREAMS OF INCOME

NOTES

MULTIPLE STREAMS OF INCOME

_____

_____

_____

_____

_____

_____

_____

_____

_____

_____

_____ MULTIPLE STREAMS OF INCOME

NOTES

MULTIPLE STREAMS OF INCOME

_____

_____

_____

_____

_____

_____

_____

_____

_____

_____

_____

NOTES

MULTIPLE STREAMS OF INCOME

NOTES

MULTIPLE STREAMS OF INCOME

_____

_____

_____

_____

_____

_____

_____

_____

_____

_____

_____

_____ MULTIPLE STREAMS OF INCOME

NOTES

MULTIPLE STREAMS OF INCOME

NOTES

MULTIPLE STREAMS OF INCOME

_____

_____

_____

_____

_____

_____

_____

_____

_____

_____

_____

_____

_____ MULTIPLE STREAMS OF INCOME

NOTES

MULTIPLE STREAMS OF INCOME

_____

_____

_____

_____

_____

_____

_____

_____

_____

_____

_____

_____ MULTIPLE STREAMS OF INCOME

NOTES

MULTIPLE STREAMS OF INCOME

NOTES

MULTIPLE STREAMS OF INCOME

_____

_____

_____

_____

_____

_____

_____

_____

_____

_____

_____

_____

_____ MULTIPLE STREAMS OF INCOME

NOTES

MULTIPLE STREAMS OF INCOME

NOTES

MULTIPLE STREAMS OF INCOME

_____

_____

_____

_____

_____

_____

_____

_____

_____

_____

_____

_____

NOTES

MULTIPLE STREAMS OF INCOME

_____
_____
_____
_____
_____
_____
_____
_____
_____
_____
_____
_____

NOTES

MULTIPLE STREAMS OF INCOME

_____

_____

_____

_____

_____

_____

_____

_____

_____

_____

_____

_____

_____ MULTIPLE STREAMS OF INCOME

NOTES

MULTIPLE STREAMS OF INCOME

NOTES

MULTIPLE STREAMS OF INCOME

--------------------------------- MULTIPLE STREAMS OF INCOME

NOTES

MULTIPLE STREAMS OF INCOME

NOTES

MULTIPLE STREAMS OF INCOME

NOTES

MULTIPLE STREAMS OF INCOME

_____

_____

_____

_____

_____

_____

_____

_____

_____

_____

_____

_____

ABOUT *The* AUTHOR

MEET THE MIND
BEHIND THE METHOD
HTTPS://LINKTR.EE/TRAYSEAN

AS HEARD ON RADIO & AS SEEN ON TV & IN NEWSPAPERS & MAGAZINES

Purpose: To eradicate poverty by teaching 1 million young people financial education

Tray-Sean Salmi Harrow:
https://www.harrowschoolonline.org/news-and-events/blogs/posts/~board/blogs/post/harrow-school-online-pupil-tray-sean-ben-salmi-wins-young-innovator-award

Harrow testimonial:
https://www.instagram.com/p/ChmfSeqM4SY/?igshid=MDJmNzVkMjY=

I'm That KID - Teaching Teens How To Trade is a grassroots project that aims to teaching teens how to trade stocked and shares.

Arabian Business article:
https://www.arabianbusiness.com/opinion/how-to-get-your-personal-finances-under-control-through-four-key-pillars

5 years trading experience (mentored by Juergen Pallien)

17yr old Tray-Sean Ben Salmi is a proud Harrovian, TEDx Speaker: Tray-Sean Ben Salmi: Financial Education is Kids' Stuff | TED Talk, Guest Speaker at the Steve & Marjorie Harvey Foundation: https://theharveyfoundation.org, an Amazon #1 Best Seller & Award-Winning Author, Award winning Public Speaker (Virgin, The Beat You Expo 15,000 attendees) and Child Advocate. Tray-Sean participated in Channel 4 Child Genius 2017 and went on to be recognized as one of the top 20 smartest children in the UK. Tray-Sean went on to be 1 out of 34 boys to be invited to sit papers at the prestigious Eton College 2017.

Tray-Sean Ben Salmi is a proud Harrovians as of 2021

Tray-Sean is founder of Influencer Publishing House.

Tray-Sean hosted his signature program called I'm That KID at Virgin Money Lounge.

Tray-Sean has recently signed a contract with FirstPoint USA   for an opportunity to go to America for a full academic and sports scholarship.

Tray-Sean was a guest speaker at The Beat You Expo: https://youtu.be/Fz9mErJC8rA where there were 15,000 attendees.

STAY
CONNECTED
HTTPS://LINKTR.EE/TRAYSEAN

Tray-Sean Ben Salmi

@authortrayseanbensalmi

info@dreamingbigtogether.com

99 LEADERS ORIGINATE IN ORDER
FOR OTHERS TO IMITATE.

THE QUESTION IS WHAT WILL YOU
CHOOSE TO DO DIFFERENTLY
NOW?...

www.ingramcontent.com/pod-product-compliance
Lightning Source LLC
Chambersburg PA
CBHW080426220326
41519CB00071BA/7210